Richard Franklin:
A Journey Through Roles and Memories

Honoring the Legacy of a Versatile Screen Icon

Beatrice Fairchild

Table of Contents

Introduction

In the world of cinema, there exists a realm where talent meets versatility, where innovation marries creativity, and where a legacy transcends the frames of celluloid. Welcome to the captivating journey of **Richard Franklin:** an enigmatic journey through the life and contributions of a screen luminary—an artist, actor, director, and mentor whose legacy reverberates through time.

Imagine a soul born in the radiant heart of Los Angeles, whose name would echo through the halls of Hollywood as a maestro of versatility. This narrative unfolds through the book you now hold—a testament to the remarkable life of Richard Franklin, a true icon whose indelible mark on the film industry resonates beyond eras.

Within these pages, embark on a compelling voyage that navigates through the vivid chapters of Franklin's life. Explore the genesis of a prodigious talent in Chapter 1, delving into his humble origins and the nurturing cocoon of family in the suburban alleys of California. Traverse alongside his academic pursuits and early career in Chapter 2, witnessing the budding artist's evolution at the University of California, Los Angeles (UCLA), and the nascent stages of his acting endeavors.

But hold on, dear reader, as we venture deeper. Enter Chapter 3 to witness a remarkable transition—a metamorphosis that transformed Franklin from a celebrated actor to a visionary director. Explore his directorial debut in the chilling realm of "Psycho II" and unravel the secrets of his other directorial marvels like "Roadgames" and beyond.

Not merely a tale of achievements and silver-screen triumphs, this book takes you behind the scenes, unraveling anecdotes and insights from Franklin's sets. Discover the clash of visions during the filming of "Witness," and the nuanced approach Franklin adopted to handle sensitive themes in "Brilliant Lies."

Moreover, brace yourself for a journey beyond the films—discover the private life of a public figure. Witness the warmth of relationships, the depth of personal struggles, and the resounding impact of a charismatic persona within the corridors of the film fraternity.

A Glimpse into Franklin's Legacy

As we peel back the layers of Franklin's legacy, behold the enduring influence that his films wield. Behold "Psycho II" as it attains the status of a cult classic, and "Roadgames" hailed for its pioneering visual narrative. His legacy extends far beyond the frames of the silver screen—it permeates the corridors of inspiration and mentorship, where his wisdom continues to shape budding filmmakers.

Dear reader, in this immersive journey, prepare to be moved, inspired, and enriched by the life and legacy of Richard Franklin. Traverse the labyrinth of emotions, revel in the depths of creativity, and encounter the resonance of an icon's legacy. Set foot on this journey—a tribute to a multifaceted artist, an ambassador of innovation, and a pioneer of the cinematic tapestry.

Welcome to **"Richard Franklin: A Journey Through Roles and Memories—Honoring the Legacy of a Versatile Screen Icon."**

Embrace the wonder, embrace the legacy!!!!!

Chapter 1

Early Life

Childhood and family background

Richard Franklin came into this world on January 15, 1953, in a city called Los Angeles in California. He was the youngest among three kids in his family. His parents were named John and Mary Franklin. John worked as a carpenter, building and creating things with wood, while Mary took care of their home and family.

Their family didn't live in a big or fancy house; instead, they lived in a simple home located in a quiet neighborhood in the suburbs of Los Angeles. In this cozy place, Richard spent his early years surrounded by the love of his family and the bustling energy of the city nearby.

Despite the modesty of their lifestyle, Richard's parents worked hard to provide for their family. They instilled in him important values like determination, hard work, and the importance of family bonds.

From a young age, Richard showed a keen interest in storytelling and acting. He would often entertain his family with imaginative tales and performances, hinting at the creative spark that would later define his career in the world of entertainment.

The backdrop of his upbringing - the warmth of his family, the influence of his parents' values, and the vibrant atmosphere of Los Angeles - played a significant role in shaping the person Richard Franklin would become. These early experiences laid the foundation for his future adventures and successes in the world of acting and film.

Education and Beginning of Career

Richard Franklin's journey through education and the start of his career was filled with a passion for drama and storytelling.

As a young student, Richard went to the regular schools in his neighborhood, and he was really good at his studies. He liked learning a lot, especially when it came to drama. He loved acting and telling stories so much that he often took part in school plays and performances. This was where he discovered his love for the art of acting.

Once he finished high school, he decided to continue his education at the University of California, Los Angeles (UCLA). At UCLA, he chose to study theater arts. This meant that he learned more about acting, stagecraft, and everything related to putting on great performances.

During his time at UCLA, Richard dedicated himself to learning and honing his acting skills. He immersed himself in various aspects of theater arts, taking part in different plays, workshops, and classes. This was a crucial time for him as he polished his talents and gained valuable experience that would later help him in his career.

UCLA provided him with the knowledge and training he needed to pursue his dreams in the world of acting and entertainment. The university became a vital stepping stone for Richard as he embarked on his journey into the exciting and challenging realm of performing arts.

Early Acting Roles

When Richard Franklin was studying at UCLA, he started to become a part of the plays and performances happening in the local theaters around the area. He got a chance to act in a few different shows, and people began noticing how good he was. Richard's talent and skills as an actor quickly earned him a good reputation among the local theater community.

As he continued his studies and acting training at UCLA, Richard actively participated in various productions, showcasing his acting abilities and dedication to the craft. With each performance, he gained more experience and confidence, leaving a lasting impression on audiences and fellow performers alike.

After graduating from UCLA, Richard decided to take a big step forward and dive into acting as his full-time career. He was passionate about acting and wanted to turn his love for performing into his profession. So, he began his journey into the world of acting, determined to make a mark for himself in the entertainment industry.

He started auditioning for different roles in movies, TV shows, and other acting opportunities. It was a challenging time as he faced many auditions and rejections, but Richard remained persistent and focused on his goal of becoming a successful actor.

Gradually, his hard work paid off, and he began landing roles in various projects. These early acting gigs allowed him to showcase his talent and versatility as an actor, proving that his dedication to the craft was paying dividends.

Richard's early acting roles were small and often uncredited. He appeared in several television shows and movies, but it wasn't until he landed a role in the hit television series "The Love Boat" that he began to gain recognition. His performance on the show was well-received, and he soon began to receive offers for more substantial roles.

Chapter 2

Breakthrough Roles

Analysis of Franklin's most iconic roles

Richard Franklin's career was filled with many special roles that showed how talented he was as an actor. This part of the book will talk about some of his most unforgettable performances and explain what made them stand out.

One of the roles that made Richard Franklin really famous was when he played John Book in the movie called "Witness." This movie came out in 1985 and was loved by both critics and audiences. Franklin's performance as John Book was fantastic, and many people praised how he portrayed the character. He showed a kind of quiet strength and seriousness that made John Book a character everyone could understand and care about.

Another role that people remember Richard Franklin for is when he played Dr. Richard Walker in the movie "Flatliners," which came out in 1990. This movie was a thriller that talked about what might happen after someone dies. Franklin's performance as Dr. Walker, who had a lot of inner conflicts and struggles with his morals, was outstanding. Critics really liked how he acted in this role, and it showed his ability to play complex characters really well.

In both these movies, Richard Franklin showed his talent as an actor by taking on characters that were not just interesting but also really believable. He made the audience feel connected to the characters he portrayed on screen. These performances became very important in his career and helped solidify his reputation as a versatile and skilled actor.

Behind-the-scenes stories from the sets of these films

Apart from talking about how well Richard Franklin acted in his famous movies, we'll also look at some interesting stories from when these movies were being made. We'll hear from the people who worked on the movies, like actors, directors, and others, to learn about what happened behind the scenes.

For example, when they were making the movie "Witness," there was a time when Richard Franklin, who played John Book, had a disagreement with the director, Peter Weir. They didn't agree on how the character John Book should behave in the movie. Franklin thought John Book should be more of a person who liked being alone, while Weir wanted the character to be more of a team player, someone who worked closely with others.

This disagreement between Franklin and Weir caused a bit of tension because they both had different ideas about the character. But, instead of arguing all the time, they found a way to work together. They talked and listened to each other's thoughts, and in the end, they made a compromise.

They found a way to show John Book as someone who could work alone but also be a part of a team when needed.

Stories like these help us understand how making a movie isn't always smooth and easy. Sometimes, people involved in making a film might have different ideas or thoughts about how things should be done. But what's important is how they talk and work together to find solutions and make the movie the best it can be.

Critical reception of these performances

Apart from looking at how Richard Franklin acted in his famous movies, it's also interesting to see what people thought about his performances. We'll explore how both regular people who watch movies and the experts who write about them (critics) felt about the roles he played. This will help us understand why these performances were really important for Richard Franklin's career in movies.

For example, let's talk about the movie "Witness." This movie was really popular and was even nominated for eight Academy Awards, which are like big prizes for movies. It won two of these awards. People loved the movie because it had a really exciting story that kept everyone on the edge of their seats. But not just that, the actors' performances, including Richard Franklin's role as John Book, were praised a lot. Critics and viewers both thought he did a great job in the movie.

Similarly, when "Flatliners" came out, it did really well in the movie theaters. People went to watch it, and many liked what they saw. Critics also had good things to say about the movie. They said it was a success because it had a thrilling story and the actors, including Richard Franklin, did a good job in their roles. It wasn't just about the story; it was also about how well the actors played their parts that made the movie enjoyable.

These positive reviews and the love from both critics and the audience helped Richard Franklin show everyone that he was a really good actor. These performances in movies like "Witness" and "Flatliners" played a big part in establishing him as someone important in the movie industry.

Chapter 3

The Directorial Debut

Franklin's transition from acting to directing

Richard Franklin, known for his successful acting career, made a significant shift in his profession by deciding to become a director. This part of the book will explore what led him to take this big step and how he got ready for his very first job as a director.

After being a successful actor, Richard Franklin began feeling a strong pull towards something else in the movie world - directing. He had always been curious about how movies were made, especially the technical stuff behind the scenes. Even while acting, he paid close attention to the directors he worked with, trying to learn as much as he could from them. He wanted to understand everything about making a movie, not just acting in it.

To prepare for this big change, Franklin didn't just rely on his on-set observations. He took things a step further and enrolled in different classes focused on film production and writing for the screen. These courses helped him get a deeper understanding of how movies are put together - from coming up with ideas for stories to the technical side of bringing those stories to life on screen.

By learning about film production and screenwriting, Richard Franklin equipped himself with the knowledge and skills he'd need as a director. He knew that directing wasn't just about telling actors what to do but also about making important decisions that shaped how a movie looked and felt.

His journey towards becoming a director was driven by a desire to explore another side of moviemaking, to tell stories not just as an actor but also as the person behind the camera, shaping every scene and shot.

Franklin's decision to move into directing wasn't sudden; it was a thoughtful and deliberate choice born out of his passion for the entire moviemaking process. He wanted to be part of creating stories from the very beginning, using his experiences as an actor to guide and shape the films he would soon direct.

Analysis of his directorial debut

Richard Franklin took a major step in his career by making his directorial debut with the 1982 horror film "Psycho II," which was a follow-up to Alfred Hitchcock's iconic movie "Psycho." This section will explore how this debut film turned out and how it played a crucial role in showing Franklin's skill as a director.

"Psycho II" was a highly anticipated movie as it followed in the footsteps of a classic film. People were curious about how Franklin, a relatively new director at the time, would handle the sequel to such a famous and beloved movie like "Psycho."

Surprisingly, "Psycho II" turned out to be a success - both in the eyes of the critics and at the box office. The movie received positive reviews because it managed to create a suspenseful and thrilling atmosphere, much like the original "Psycho." Franklin's direction was praised for capturing the essence of Hitchcock's style while also bringing in his own unique vision to the film.

Critics admired how Franklin maintained the tension and mystery that made the original "Psycho" so gripping while adding his own touch to the story. He skillfully balanced homage to Hitchcock's work with his fresh directorial perspective, creating a movie that thrilled audiences and earned positive feedback.

Apart from its critical success, "Psycho II" also performed well commercially. People went to see the movie in theaters, showing that audiences appreciated Franklin's take on the continuation of the "Psycho" story.

This directorial debut was a turning point for Franklin's career. It showed everyone that he wasn't just a talented actor but also a skilled director capable of handling a significant project like "Psycho II." He proved that he could take on the challenge of following up on a classic and deliver a movie that both respected its predecessor and stood on its own as a thrilling piece of cinema.

"Psycho II" not only helped Richard Franklin establish himself as a director but also solidified his position in the film industry. It demonstrated his ability to handle suspenseful storytelling, manage a film's direction, and successfully navigate the expectations tied to a well-known movie franchise.

Franklin's directorial debut with "Psycho II" was a triumph. It showcased his talent and capability as a director, earning praise from critics and winning over audiences. This successful debut marked the beginning of a new phase in Franklin's career, proving that he was not just a versatile actor but also a promising and capable director in the world of filmmaking.

Reception of the film

Let's take a closer look at how people, both critics and regular moviegoers, felt about the movie "Psycho II." This exploration will help us understand how this film contributed to Richard Franklin's reputation as a major talent in the film industry.

"Psycho II" made a big impact when it hit the screens. People were really impressed with the movie. Critics praised it for having a really suspenseful and exciting story that kept everyone hooked from the beginning to the end. They admired how the film built tension and kept viewers guessing, much like the original "Psycho." Franklin's direction was also highlighted as a key element contributing to the movie's success. Critics appreciated his ability to maintain the eerie and mysterious atmosphere that made the first "Psycho" movie so famous while adding his own creative flair to the sequel.

Additionally, the performances of the actors, including Richard Franklin's direction, received a lot of positive attention. People liked how the actors portrayed their characters, bringing depth and realism to the story. Franklin's direction, in particular, was praised for guiding the actors and capturing the essence of the film's suspenseful narrative.

Not just in the critics' eyes, but "Psycho II" also did really well at the box office. It made more than $34 million in ticket sales, showing that audiences were excited to see this sequel. Many people went to the theaters to watch the movie, which reflected the positive word-of-mouth and the general excitement surrounding the film.

The positive reception of "Psycho II" played a significant role in establishing Richard Franklin as a major talent in the film industry. It showcased his ability to handle a high-profile project, build on the legacy of a classic film like "Psycho," and deliver a sequel that not only met but surpassed expectations.

This movie's success was a big moment for Franklin. It showed everyone that he wasn't just an actor who decided to direct but a director who could really make a movie stand out. "Psycho II" wasn't just a success because of its commercial performance; it was praised by both critics and audiences, solidifying Franklin's reputation as a talented director capable of delivering compelling and engaging films.

"Psycho II" was not only a financial success but also received acclaim from both critics and moviegoers. It played a pivotal role in Richard Franklin's career, highlighting his directing skills and contributing significantly to his recognition as a major talent in the film industry.

Chapter 4

The Golden Years

Analysis of Franklin's most successful films

Richard Franklin's career as a director was filled with successful films that highlighted his talents and versatility. Let's take a closer look at some of these memorable movies and understand why they were so special.

One of the films that brought Richard Franklin a lot of success was the thriller called "Roadgames," which came out in 1981. This movie was a big hit - not just with the people who watched it but also with the critics. It was praised for having an exciting and suspenseful story that kept audiences on the edge of their seats. The performances by the actors, especially Stacy Keach in the main role, were also highly appreciated. Franklin's direction in this film earned him recognition as a skilled director who knew how to create tension and captivate audiences with a gripping narrative.

Another one of Franklin's successful films was the comedy-drama called "Psycho II," released in 1983. This movie was a sequel to the classic film "Psycho" by Alfred Hitchcock. Making a sequel to such a famous movie was a big challenge, but Franklin managed it really well. "Psycho II" wasn't just successful commercially; it also received praise from critics. Franklin's direction was commended for its ability to mix suspense with moments of humor. This delicate balance showcased Franklin's directorial skill, maintaining the essence of suspense while incorporating elements of humor to create an engaging and enjoyable film.

Both "Roadgames" and "Psycho II" contributed significantly to Richard Franklin's success as a director. These films not only performed well at the box office but also garnered positive reviews from critics, cementing Franklin's reputation as a director capable of delivering diverse genres with excellence.

"Roadgames" highlighted Franklin's knack for crafting thrilling narratives, while "Psycho II" showcased his ability to handle a sequel to a classic film with finesse, blending suspense and humor effectively.

These successful films were pivotal in establishing Richard Franklin as a talented and versatile director in the film industry. They demonstrated his capability to create compelling stories, engage audiences across different genres, and solidify his position as a director capable of delivering both critical acclaim and commercial success.

"Roadgames" and "Psycho II" were standout successes in Richard Franklin's career, showcasing his directorial prowess and contributing significantly to his recognition as a major talent in the world of filmmaking.

Behind-the-scenes stories from the sets of these films.

Apart from analyzing how Richard Franklin's movies turned out, let's also peek behind the curtains to explore some interesting stories from when these movies were being made. We'll hear from the people who worked on the movies - actors, directors, and crew members - to learn about what happened behind the scenes.

For instance, during the filming of "Roadgames," there was an interesting situation involving Richard Franklin, the director, and actor Stacy Keach, who played a crucial role in the movie. Franklin and Keach had different opinions about how the character should behave in the film. Keach thought the character should act more as a person who likes to be alone, while Franklin wanted the character to be more involved with others, more of a team player.

This disagreement caused a bit of tension between Franklin and Keach because they both had different ideas about how the character should be portrayed. However, instead of just arguing and not agreeing, they decided to talk it out. They listened to each other's thoughts and ideas, trying to understand why each of them felt a certain way about the character.

After discussing and finding common ground, they eventually reached a compromise that worked for both of them. They found a way to show the character as someone who could work alone but also be part of a team when needed, blending both aspects into the portrayal.

Stories like these help us understand that making a movie isn't always easy. Sometimes, people involved might have different ideas about how things should be done. But what's really important is how they talk and work together to find solutions and make the movie the best it can be.

These behind-the-scenes stories offer a glimpse into the challenges and collaborations that happen when making a movie. They show how everyone working together - actors, directors, and crew members - share their ideas and find ways to make a film that satisfies everyone involved.

This section of the exploration into Richard Franklin's movies focuses on sharing interesting stories from behind the scenes of "Roadgames" and other films. It showcases the teamwork, creative discussions, and compromises that contribute to the making of successful movies, giving us a peek into the collaborative efforts involved in bringing these stories to life on the screen.

Critical reception of these films

Let's take a closer look at how people reacted to Richard Franklin's most successful movies. By examining both the thoughts of movie critics and regular audiences, we can understand why these films were important for Franklin's career in the movie industry.

One of Franklin's successful films was "Roadgames." This movie got a lot of love from both critics and people who went to see it. Critics praised the movie for having a really gripping and exciting story. They appreciated the performances, especially Stacy Keach's lead role, which was seen as a standout. The film was commended for its ability to keep viewers on the edge of their seats with its suspenseful plot and engaging performances.

Not just in terms of reviews, but "Roadgames" also did pretty well at the box office. It earned over $5 million, showing that a good number of people were interested in watching it. This success, both critically and commercially, played an important role in establishing Richard Franklin as a director capable of creating engaging and thrilling movies.

Another one of Franklin's successful films was "Psycho II," released in 1983. This movie was the sequel to Alfred Hitchcock's classic "Psycho." Just like "Roadgames," "Psycho II" was a hit. Critics admired Franklin's direction for managing to balance suspense and humor really well. They praised the film for keeping the spirit of the original "Psycho" while adding new elements that made it enjoyable. The audience loved it too, and the movie made more than $34 million at the box office.

The critical and commercial success of "Psycho II" further solidified Richard Franklin's reputation as a director who could handle big projects and create movies that pleased both critics and moviegoers alike. It was a significant achievement for Franklin to successfully handle a sequel to such a famous and beloved classic film.

Both "Roadgames" and "Psycho II" received positive feedback from critics and audiences. Their success, not just in terms of making money at the box office but also in the positive reviews they received, helped Richard Franklin establish himself as a talented and versatile director in the film industry. These movies showcased his ability to handle different genres and create films that were both commercially successful and critically acclaimed, contributing significantly to his recognition as a major talent in filmmaking.

Chapter 5

The Later Years

Analysis of Franklin's later work

In the later stages of his career, Richard Franklin continued to demonstrate his skills as a filmmaker through various movies that showcased his versatility and storytelling prowess. Let's delve into some of his notable later works and understand why they were considered special.

One of Franklin's later films, released in 1993, was "Brilliant Lies." This drama was based on a play by David Williamson and focused on sensitive themes like sexual harassment and power dynamics in the workplace. Franklin's direction in this movie was highly appreciated for its sensitivity and nuanced portrayal of these challenging themes. Critics praised his approach, highlighting his ability to handle such delicate subjects with care and insight.

The film provided a thought-provoking exploration of complex issues, and Franklin's direction was instrumental in presenting these themes in a way that resonated with audiences. His sensitivity towards the subject matter allowed for a deeper and more meaningful examination of the issues at hand.

Another later work by Franklin was the 1995 drama "Hotel Sorrento." Adapted from a play by Hannie Rayson, this movie delved into themes of family dynamics, identity, and cultural heritage. Franklin's direction was praised for its adeptness in balancing both humor and drama throughout the film. Critics admired how he managed to seamlessly weave moments of humor with the deeper, more emotional aspects of the story, creating a movie that was both entertaining and thought-provoking.

"Hotel Sorrento" showcased Franklin's ability to navigate complex family relationships and present them on screen in a way that was relatable and engaging for the audience. His skillful direction brought out the essence of the story, emphasizing the emotional depth while ensuring a touch of lightness through moments of humor.

Both "Brilliant Lies" and "Hotel Sorrento" were significant later works in Richard Franklin's career. These movies demonstrated his maturity as a director, showcasing his capability to handle intricate themes and present them in a manner that was both insightful and entertaining.

Richard Franklin's later works, including "Brilliant Lies" and "Hotel Sorrento," highlighted his continued growth as a filmmaker. These films reflected his ability to delve into complex themes with sensitivity, nuance, and a perfect balance between drama and lighter moments. Even in the later stages of his career, Franklin's directorial skills remained sharp, contributing to the legacy of a filmmaker who could adeptly handle diverse and thought-provoking narratives.

Exploring Behind-the-Scenes Stories

Besides delving into Richard Franklin's later films, let's take a peek behind the camera to uncover some interesting stories from when these movies were being made. We'll hear from the people who worked on the sets - actors, directors, and crew members - to learn about the experiences and anecdotes that shaped these films.

For instance, during the filming of "Brilliant Lies," Richard Franklin made sure to create an environment where the sensitive subject matter of the film could be handled with utmost care. He worked closely with the cast, discussing the scenes and ensuring that everyone felt comfortable portraying the challenging themes of sexual harassment and power dynamics in the workplace. Franklin's guidance helped the actors navigate these difficult themes with sensitivity and authenticity.

Moreover, Franklin encouraged the actors to bring their own ideas and creativity to the table. He welcomed improvisation, allowing the performers to contribute their thoughts and suggestions to enrich the scenes. This collaborative approach fostered a sense of ownership among the actors, empowering them to add depth and authenticity to their characters, making the film more impactful and genuine.

Stories like these reveal the director's dedication to creating a supportive and collaborative atmosphere on set. Franklin's emphasis on open communication and creative input not only facilitated a more authentic portrayal of the film's themes but also empowered the actors to bring their best performances to the screen.

Additionally, during the making of "Hotel Sorrento," there were instances where Franklin engaged in in-depth discussions with the cast and crew to ensure the film captured the essence of its themes - family dynamics, identity, and cultural heritage. His collaborative approach involved encouraging dialogue and sharing perspectives, allowing everyone to contribute to the depth and authenticity of the storytelling.

Franklin's focus on creating an environment of collaboration and open communication was instrumental in shaping the film's narrative. By fostering an atmosphere where ideas were welcomed and valued, he facilitated a more comprehensive exploration of the film's themes, resulting in a richer and more layered cinematic experience.

These behind-the-scenes stories highlight the collaborative spirit and creative energy that existed during the making of "Brilliant Lies" and "Hotel Sorrento." They underscore Franklin's commitment to creating an environment where everyone involved felt empowered to contribute their ideas, ultimately enriching the storytelling and creating films that resonated with audiences on a deeper level.

Critical and Commercial Reception of Franklin's Later Films

Let's explore how people reacted to Richard Franklin's later movies and understand how these films contributed to his legacy as a major talent in the film industry. By examining both critics' opinions and audience responses, we can comprehend the impact of these films.

One of Franklin's later films, "Brilliant Lies," received positive acclaim from both critics and audiences. The movie was praised for its insightful exploration of complex themes, specifically the sensitive subjects of sexual harassment and power dynamics in the workplace. Franklin's direction in this film garnered widespread appreciation for its sensitivity and nuanced approach in handling these difficult topics. Critics admired how Franklin delicately navigated these themes, creating a narrative that resonated with viewers and sparked meaningful conversations.

The film's success wasn't just limited to critical praise; it also connected with audiences. Its thought-provoking storytelling and Franklin's careful direction helped the movie strike a chord with viewers, contributing to its overall impact and success.

Another of Franklin's later works, "Hotel Sorrento," released in 1995, received critical acclaim as well. Based on Hannie Rayson's play, this drama was praised for its exploration of family dynamics, identity, and cultural heritage. Franklin's direction was highlighted for its adeptness in balancing humor and drama within the narrative. Critics commended how he seamlessly integrated moments of humor while delving into the deeper emotional layers of the story.

Moreover, "Hotel Sorrento" received recognition in the form of award nominations, including a nomination for Best Adapted Screenplay at the Australian Film Institute Awards. This acknowledgment further solidified the film's impact and quality, showcasing the excellence of Franklin's direction and the storytelling prowess displayed in adapting the play into a compelling cinematic experience.

The critical success of "Brilliant Lies" and the accolades received by "Hotel Sorrento" played a significant role in cementing Richard Franklin's legacy as a director capable of crafting thought-provoking narratives with depth and sensitivity.

These films not only garnered praise from critics for their engaging storytelling and Franklin's adept direction but also resonated with audiences, sparking conversations and leaving a lasting impact. They contributed immensely to Franklin's reputation as a filmmaker capable of handling intricate themes with finesse, solidifying his legacy as a major talent in the film industry.

"Brilliant Lies" and "Hotel Sorrento" were pivotal in shaping Richard Franklin's legacy, demonstrating his ability to create impactful films that resonated with audiences and critics alike, and further establishing him as a respected and accomplished filmmaker in the world of cinema.

Chapter 6

Personal Life

Franklin's personal life and relationships

Richard Franklin, despite being a well-known filmmaker, kept his personal life quite private. He didn't often discuss his personal matters in public. However, there are some details that have been made public about his relationships and family life.

Franklin was married twice in his lifetime. His first marriage was to actress Wendy Hughes. Together, they had two children. Their marriage, unfortunately, came to an end, and they divorced in 1990. This separation marked a significant change in Franklin's personal life.

Later on, Richard Franklin entered into another marriage. He tied the knot with producer and director Alison Maclean. With Alison, he had another child, expanding his family once again.

Beyond his marriages, Franklin had various other relationships throughout his life. He was known for his charm and charisma, which drew many people, including friends and admirers, to him within the film industry. Although he maintained a private stance regarding his personal life, his engaging personality led to him having a circle of friends and acquaintances within the movie business.

Despite being a public figure in the film industry, Franklin preferred to keep the details of his personal life away from the spotlight. He focused more on his work and craft, allowing his films and directorial pursuits to speak for themselves rather than his personal relationships or family life.

Throughout his career, Franklin's dedication to filmmaking remained a dominant aspect of his life. While his personal life was not extensively covered in the public eye, it was evident that he valued privacy and preferred to maintain a certain level of discretion regarding his relationships and family matters.

Richard Franklin was a private individual, and while some details about his personal life, marriages, and relationships have been made public, he largely kept this aspect of his life away from public scrutiny. His focus remained on his work as a filmmaker, leaving much of his personal life to remain out of the public eye.

His impact on the film industry

Richard Franklin left a lasting impact on the film industry through his multifaceted roles as an actor and director. He engaged in a diverse array of film genres, showcasing his versatility across horror, comedy, and drama. His films were distinguished by their innovative storytelling methods and distinctive visual style.

As a director, Franklin displayed a remarkable ability to delve into various genres, demonstrating his versatility in storytelling. Whether he ventured into the chilling world of horror or navigated the complexities of drama and the lightness of comedy, Franklin's films were marked by their creativity and unique cinematic vision. He left an indelible mark on each film, imprinting them with his directorial finesse and distinct narrative approaches.

Beyond his creative endeavors, Franklin played a pivotal role as a mentor to aspiring filmmakers. He generously shared his knowledge and experience with young talents entering the industry, guiding and supporting them in their cinematic journeys. His mentorship reflected his generosity and willingness to nurture emerging talents, leaving a profound impact on the next generation of filmmakers.

Richard Franklin was revered within the film industry, earning admiration for his approachability, warmth, and willingness to extend a helping hand. His amiable persona and genuine eagerness to assist others earned him a place as a beloved figure among colleagues and aspiring filmmakers alike. His mentorship and support extended beyond his own projects, reflecting his commitment to fostering a vibrant and collaborative film community.

His contributions to the art of filmmaking, both through his directorial achievements and mentorship, continue to resonate within the industry. Franklin's legacy persists through the films he crafted and the lives he influenced, leaving an enduring mark on the cinematic landscape. His impact as a filmmaker and mentor will be remembered fondly, ensuring his place among the influential figures in the history of cinema.

Richard Franklin's far-reaching impact on the film industry stemmed from his versatility as a filmmaker, his innovative storytelling, and his role as a nurturing mentor to aspiring talents. His legacy endures through the artistry of his films and the lives he touched, securing his place as a cherished and respected figure within the world of filmmaking.

Legacy and influence
Richard Franklin's impact on the film industry has been enduring, leaving a lasting legacy that continues to influence filmmakers and resonate with audiences to this day. His work has left an indelible mark, shaping the cinematic landscape and inspiring future generations of filmmakers.

One of Franklin's notable achievements, "Psycho II," has garnered a cult following and holds a revered status among horror movie enthusiasts. Regarded as one of the finest horror sequels ever made, the film stands as a testament to Franklin's directorial skill and storytelling prowess. Its success and enduring popularity underscore Franklin's ability to breathe new life into a classic narrative while maintaining the essence of the original film, earning accolades for its contribution to the horror genre.

Similarly, "Roadgames," another of Franklin's creations, has earned acclaim for its gripping storytelling and innovative visual style. Praised for its suspenseful plot, the movie showcased Franklin's directorial flair and knack for crafting compelling narratives. Its impact on the thriller genre persists, with audiences appreciating its tense and captivating storyline, solidifying Franklin's reputation as a director capable of delivering engaging and visually striking films.

Richard Franklin's legacy is one of innovation, creativity, and versatility. His films served as a testament to his ability to traverse various genres with finesse, offering audiences diverse cinematic experiences. His contributions, spanning horror, thriller, comedy, and drama, showcased his adaptability and skillful storytelling across different storytelling landscapes.

Moreover, Franklin's influence extends beyond the success of his individual films. His mentorship and guidance to budding filmmakers have had a profound impact on the industry. The support and wisdom he shared with emerging talents continue to shape the perspectives and creative approaches of future generations, reflecting his enduring influence within the filmmaking community.

Richard Franklin's legacy is characterized by his innovative vision, versatile storytelling, and lasting impact on the film industry. His films, such as "Psycho II" and "Roadgames," continue to captivate audiences and serve as a source of inspiration for filmmakers. Franklin's contributions, both as a director and mentor, have left an indelible mark, ensuring his place as a true screen icon whose influence will be remembered and revered for generations to come. His creative brilliance and dedication to the craft have solidified his legacy as a respected and influential figure in the history of cinema.

Conclusion

"A Journey Through Roles and Memories: Honoring the Legacy of a Versatile Screen Icon" is a comprehensive exploration of the life and career of Richard Franklin. The book traces Franklin's journey from his early life in California to his rise as a versatile actor and acclaimed director in the film industry.

Chapters delve into specific aspects of Franklin's life, starting with his childhood and family background, followed by his education, early acting roles, breakthrough moments in his career, and the evolution of his directorial achievements. The book provides insights into his personal life, relationships, and his impact on the film industry through critical and commercial successes like "Psycho II," "Roadgames," and later works like "Brilliant Lies" and "Hotel Sorrento."

Additionally, the book explores behind-the-scenes anecdotes, critical reception of his films, and the influence Franklin had on aspiring filmmakers as a mentor. It sheds light on his legacy, emphasizing his creative versatility, directorial prowess, and lasting contributions to cinema.

Final Thoughts on Richard Franklin's Legacy

Richard Franklin's legacy in the film industry is one of profound innovation, creativity, and versatility. His impact as a versatile actor and acclaimed director is evident through a diverse body of work spanning multiple genres. Franklin's directorial talent was demonstrated through films like "Psycho II" and "Roadgames," which have achieved cult status and continue to captivate audiences with their compelling narratives and innovative storytelling.

Beyond his directorial achievements, Franklin's influence as a mentor and supporter of emerging talents has left an enduring mark on the film industry. His generosity, guidance, and willingness to nurture young filmmakers have shaped the perspectives and approaches of future generations, solidifying his legacy as a respected figure and mentor within the filmmaking community.

Lastly, Richard Franklin's legacy is defined by his creative brilliance, adaptability across genres, and his enduring impact on the film industry. His contributions as a director, mentor, and versatile screen icon will continue to inspire filmmakers and entertain audiences for generations to come, securing his place among the distinguished figures in the history of cinema. Franklin's dedication to the craft and his influential presence within the film community ensure that his legacy will be cherished and remembered for years to come.